*Gardens*

*of*

*Friendship*

*Loyal friendship*
*Pure and true* ✝
*Such is what*
*I feel for you.*

*To*

_____

*From*

_____

*Date*

_____

# Ribbons of Love

### GARDENS OF FRIENDSHIP

### HAPPY IS THE HOUSE
*That Shelters a Friend*

### IN THE PRESENCE OF ANGELS

### JUST FOR YOU
*A Celebration of Joy and Friendship*

### LOVING THOUGHTS
*for Tender Hearts*

### MOTHER
*Another Word for Love*

# Gardens

# of

# Friendship

Edited by Paul C. Brownlow

*Brownlow*

Brownlow Publishing Company, Inc.

*Blessed is the man who has*

*the gift of making friends;*

*for it is one of God's best gifts.*

*It involves many things,*

*but above all the power*

*of going out of one's own self*

*and seeing and appreciating*

*whatever is noble*

*and loving in another man.*

THOMAS HUGHES

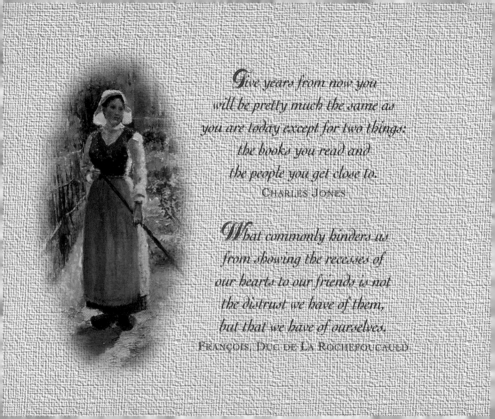

*Five years from now you
will be pretty much the same as
you are today except for two things:
the books you read and
the people you get close to.*

CHARLES JONES

*What commonly hinders us
from showing the recesses of
our hearts to our friends is not
the distrust we have of them,
but that we have of ourselves.*

FRANÇOIS, DUC DE LA ROCHEFOUCAULD

# Friend

*I would empty*
*thy chalice of heart-ache and pain,*
*Would freshen thy desert with flowers and rain,*
*Would draw out the bitter and pour in the sweet,*
*And remove every thorn from the way of thy feet;*
*Would sing in the gladness of summer and bloom,*
*And sing out the sadness of winter and gloom,*
*Would lessen thy load by enlarging thy life,*
*I would sing back repose, and*
*would sing away strife.*

CHARLES COKE WOODS

*I account that one of the greatest demonstrations of real friendship, that a friend can really endeavor to have his friend advanced in honor, in reputation, in the opinion of wit or learning, before himself.*

JEREMY TAYLOR

*Anybody can sympathize
with the sufferings of a friend,
but it requires a very fine nature to
sympathize with a friend's success.*

OSCAR WILDE

*Talk not of wasted affection;
affection never was wasted.*

HENRY WADSWORTH LONGFELLOW

*Except in cases of necessity, which are rare,
leave your friend to learn unpleasant things from
his enemies; they are ready enough to tell them.*

OLIVER WENDELL HOLMES

*Be courteous to all, but intimate with few;
and let those few be well tried before
you give them your confidence.*

GEORGE WASHINGTON

*Take out the weeds from some wild spot,*
*Remove each stone that shows,*
*Plant seeds of friendship good and deep,*
*And tend the plant that grows.*

MARY FREEMAN STARTZMAN

*A friendship will be young
after the lapse of half a century;
a passion is old at the end of three months.*

MADAME SWETCHINE

*No man or woman of the humblest sort can
really be strong, gentle, pure and good without the
world being better for it, without somebody being helped
and comforted by the very existence of that goodness.*

PHILLIPS BROOKS

*Never injure a friend, even in jest.*

CICERO

*When friends ask, there is no tomorrow.*

PROVERB

*Love is friendship set to music.*

EDWARD POLLOCK

You cannot be friends
upon any other terms
than upon the terms of equality.

WOODROW WILSON

The best way to wipe out a friendship
is to sponge on it.

Friendship adds a brighter radiance to prosperity
and lightens the burden of adversity
by dividing and sharing it.

CICERO

# From Friendship's Hand

Only a little rose, you see,
From friendship's hand I come to thee.
She plucked and said, "Go, rosebud, go,"
And then she whispered o'er me low,
"Oh, would his heart were pure tonight
As thou, dear rosebud, fresh and bright."
She whispered low, "Go, rosebud sweet,
And tell him, tho' we ne'er may meet,
An earnest prayer I'll for him send,
That God may keep him to the end."
Only a little rose, you see,
From friendship's hand I come to thee.

GEORGIA McCOY

$\mathscr{B}$eing with people you
like and respect is so meaningful.
Perhaps you have known some of them
most of your life. Having friends around for a
pleasant evening is one of life's most cherished joys
as far as I am concerned. But when those with me
are fellow believers how much greater that joy is,
for we know that it will be rekindled,
one day, in eternity.

JAMES STEWART

*I trust that even when
I'm out of sight I'm not out of mind.
Silences and distances are woven into
the texture of every true friendship.*

ROBERTA ISRAELOFF

*Friendship has certain essential characteristics
without which it is unworthy of the name.
The basis of true friendship is
self-sacrifice, disinterestedness, truth,
virtue and constancy.*

JAMES GIBBONS

# If I Had Known

How many a heart that bleeds in vain,
How many a spirit racked with pain,
Cries out —and bitter is its moan—
"If I had known! If I had known!

"I would have loved my friends more dear;
I would have prized my blessings here;
And precious seed more early sown,
If I had known! If I had known!"

M. A. KIDDER

*I would be friends with you
and have your love.*

WILLIAM SHAKESPEARE

*Be slow to fall into friendship;
but when thou art in,
continue firm and constant.*

SOCRATES

*One loyal friend is worth ten thousand relatives.*

EURIPIDES

*Better be a nettle in the side
of your friend than his echo.*

RALPH WALDO EMERSON

*A friend is one who does not laugh
when you are in a ridiculous position.*

SIR ARTHUR HELPS

*Our friendships should be immortal,
our enmities mortal.*

LIVY

# We Belong to Each Other

We all belong to each other, but friendship

is the especial accord of one life with a kindred life.

We tremble at the threshold of any new friendship

with awe and wonder and fear lest it should

not be real or, believing that it is, lest we should

prove ourselves unworthy of the solemn and

holy contact of life with life, of soul with soul.

We cannot live unworthy lives in the constant

presence of noble beings to whom we belong

and who believe that we are at least

endeavoring after nobleness.

RALPH WALDO EMERSON

*Small service is*

*true service while it lasts.*

*Of humblest friends,*

*bright creature scorn not one!*

*The daisy, by the shadow that it casts,*

*Protects the lingering dew-drop*

*from the sun.*

WILLIAM WORDSWORTH

A poor man may be said to be
rich in the midst of his poverty,
so long as he enjoys the
interior sunshine of a devoted friend.
The wealthiest of men, on the contrary,
is poor and miserable, if he has
no friend whom he can grasp
by the hand, and to whom he can
disclose the secrets of his heart.

JAMES GIBBONS

Thus nature has no love for solitude,
and always leans, as it were,
on some support; and the
sweetest support is found in the
most intimate friendship.

CICERO

The proper office of a friend
is to side with you when you are in
the wrong. Nearly anybody will side
with you when you are in the right.

MARK TWAIN

*When friends meet, hearts warm.*

PROVERB

*It brings comfort to have companions in whatever happens.*

JOHN CHRYSOSTOM

*He whose hand is clasped in friendship cannot throw mud.*

ANONYMOUS

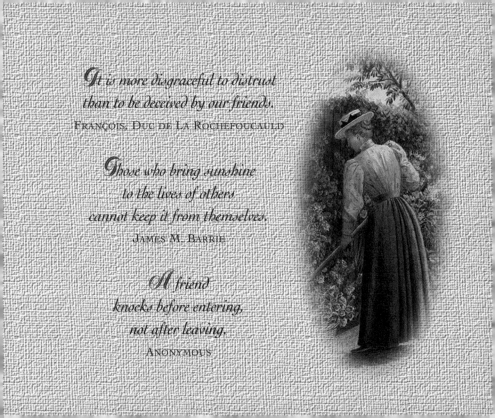

*It is more disgraceful to distrust
than to be deceived by our friends.*
FRANÇOIS, DUC DE LA ROCHEFOUCAULD

*Those who bring sunshine
to the lives of others
cannot keep it from themselves.*
JAMES M. BARRIE

*A friend
knocks before entering,
not after leaving.*
ANONYMOUS

*A friend attributed the secret of his popularity to one particular word. "Years ago," he said, "upon hearing a statement with which I disagreed, I used to say, 'Baloney,' and people began to avoid me like the plague. Now I substitute 'Amazing' for 'Baloney,' and my phone keeps ringing and my list of friends continues to grow."*

CAPPER'S WEEKLY

To be a friend
a man should go more than halfway
with his fellowmen; he should greet others
first and not wait to be greeted; he should radiate
a spirit of overflowing goodwill.

To be a friend a man should remember that we are human
magnets; that like attracts like, and that what we give we get.

To be a friend a man should recognize that no man
knows all the answers, and that he should add
each day to his knowledge of how to
live the friendly way.

WILFERD A. PETERSON

*Greater love hath no man than this,*

*that a man lay down his life for his friends.*

JOHN 15:13

*The best mirror is an old friend.*

ENGLISH PROVERB

*A friend you have to buy won't be worth*

*what you pay for him.*

GEORGE D. PRENTICE

*Those friends thou hast,*

*and their adoption tried,*

*Grapple them to thy soul with hoops of steel;*

*But do not dull thy palm with entertainment*

*Of each new-hatch'd,*

*unfledg'd comrade.*

WILLIAM SHAKESPEARE

# One Heart, One Mind

Make us of one heart and mind,

Courteous, merciful, and kind;

Lowly, meek in thought and word,

Ne'er by fretful passion stirred.

*Free from anger, free from pride,*

*Let us thus in God abide;*

*All the depth of love express,*

*All the height of holiness.*

CHARLES WESLEY

*It is a good and safe rule to sojourn in*
*every place as if you meant to spend your life there,*
*never omitting an opportunity of doing a kindness,*
*or speaking a true word, or making a friend.*

JOHN RUSKIN

*Yes, there is a talkability that can express itself*
*even without words. There is an exchange of thought*
*and feeling which is happy alike in speech and in silence.*
*It is quietness pervaded with friendship.*

HENRY VAN DYKE

When true friends

meet in adverse hour,

'Tis like a sunbeam

through a shower,

A watery way

an instant seen,

The darkly closing

clouds between.

Sir Walter Scott

*I cannot but think that the world*

*would be better and brighter if our teachers*

*would dwell on the Duty of Happiness*

*as well as on the Happiness of Duty,*

*for we ought to be as cheerful as we can,*

*if only because to be happy ourselves*

*is a most effectual contribution*

*to the happiness of others.*

SIR JOHN LUBBOCK

# Three Gates

If you are tempted to reveal
A tale to you someone has told
About another, make it pass,
Before you speak, three gates of gold.
These narrow gates: First, "Is it true?"
Then, "Is it needful?" In your mind

Give truthful answer. And the next
Is last and narrowest, "Is it kind?"
And if to reach your lips at last
It passes through these gateways three,
Then you may tell the tale, nor fear
What the result of speech may be.

FROM THE ARABIAN

*Old friends are best:*
*where can you find a new friend that has*
*stood by you as long as the old ones have?*

PROVERB

*Every man should have a fair-sized cemetery*
*in which to bury the faults of his friends.*

HENRY BROOKS ADAMS

*When two friends part they should lock up each*
*other's secrets and exchange keys. The truly*
*noble mind has no resentments.*

DIOGENES

*You may poke
a man's fire after you've
known him for seven years.*

ENGLISH PROVERB

*Grief can take care of itself,
but to get the full value of joy, you must
have a friend with whom to share it.*

*Your friend is your field which
you sow with love and
reap with thanksgiving.*

KAHLIL GIBRAN

*One recipe for friendship is the right mixture of commonality and difference. You've got to have enough in common so that you understand each other and enough difference so that there is something to exchange.*

ROBERT WEISS

*He was a friend indeed,*
*With all a friend's best virtues shining bright;*
*It was no broken reed*
*You leaned on, when you trusted in his might.*

WILLIAM HUNTER BRICKHEAD

*Among the blessings and enjoyments of this life,*

*there are few that can be compared in value*

*to the possession of a faithful friend,*

*who will pour the truth into your heart*

*though you may wince under it —*

*of a friend who will defend you when you are*

*unjustly assailed by the tongues of calumny,*

*who will not forsake you when*

*you have fallen into disgrace,*

who will counsel you in your doubts and perplexities,

who will open his purse to aid you without

expecting any return of his favors,

who will rejoice at your prosperity

and grieve at your adversity,

who will bear half of your burden —

who will add to your joys, and diminish

your sorrows by sharing in both.

JAMES GIBBONS

*If I mayn't tell you what I feel, what is the use of a friend?*

WILLIAM MAKEPEACE THACKERAY

*The greatest healing therapy is friendship and love.*

HUBERT HUMPHREY

*Friendship with oneself is all-important because without it
one cannot be friends with anyone else in the world.*

ELEANOR ROOSEVELT

*In the end we are all separate: our stories,*
*no matter how similar, come to a fork and diverge.*
*We are drawn to each other because of our similarities,*
*but it is our differences we must learn to respect.*

ROBERTA ISRAELOFF

*We take care of our health, we lay up money,*
*we make our roof tight and our clothing sufficient,*
*but who provides wisely that he shall not be wanting*
*in the best property of all—friends?*

RALPH WALDO EMERSON

*But friend to me*
*He is all fault who hath*
*no fault at all,*
*For who loves me must*
*have a touch of earth.*
ALFRED, LORD TENNYSON

*True happiness consists*
*not in the multitude*
*of friends,*
*but in their*
*worth and choice.*
SAMUEL JOHNSON

*Associate with men of good quality,*
*if you esteem your own reputation;*
*for it is better to be alone than in bad company.*

GEORGE WASHINGTON

*Chance makes our parents,*
*but choice makes our friends.*

JACQUES DELILLE

*A real friend is one who will tell you*
*of your faults and follies in prosperity,*
*and assist with his hand and heart in adversity.*

*The best way
to keep your friends
is not to give
them away.*

WILSON MIZNER

*Friendships that have
stood the test —
Time and change —
are surely best.*

JOSEPH PARRY

*The problems that*

*plague a friendship are rarely*

*one hundred percent the other person's fault.*

*We should self-examine carefully*

*before we make up our mind—*

*and before we close it.*

JUDITH VIORST

*We rejoice in
the joys of our friends as much as
we do our own, and we are equally grieved
at their sorrows. Wherefore the wise man will
feel toward his friend as he does toward himself,
and whatever labor he would encounter
with a view to his own pleasure,
he will encounter also for
the sake of his friend.*

CICERO

*The most I can do for my friend is simply to
be his friend. I have no wealth to bestow upon him.
If he knows that I am happy in loving him he will
want no other reward. Is not friendship divine in this?*

LAVATIN

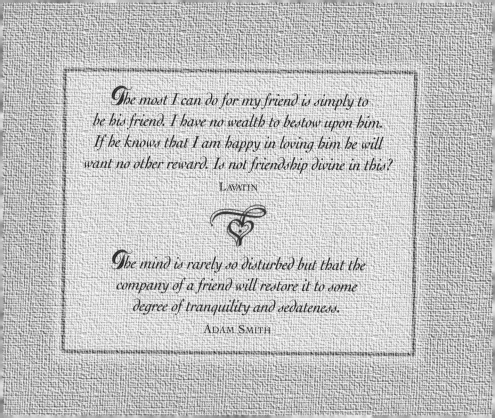

*The mind is rarely so disturbed but that the
company of a friend will restore it to some
degree of tranquility and sedateness.*

ADAM SMITH

*My best friend is the one who
brings out the best in me.*

HENRY FORD

*Part of what friends experience is something
that people who aren't friends can't know.
It's a code. It's another language.*

JUDD NELSON

*A benevolent man should allow a few faults in himself,
to keep his friends in countenance.*

BENJAMIN FRANKLIN

# I Sought My Soul

I sought my soul,

But my soul I could not see.

I sought my God,

But my God eluded me.

I sought my brother,

And I found all three.

AUTHOR UNKNOWN

*Ah, how good it feels —*

*the hand of an old friend!*

HENRY WADSWORTH LONGFELLOW

*For he, indeed, who looks into*

*the face of a friend, beholds,*

*as it were, a copy of himself.*

CICERO

# What Is a Friend?

*An English publication offered a prize for the best definition of a friend, and among the thousands of answers received were the following:*

*"One who multiplies joys, divides grief, and whose honesty is inviolable."*

"One who understands our silence."

"A volume of sympathy bound in cloth."

"A watch which beats true for all time
and never runs down."

Here is the definition that won the prize:

"A friend is the one who comes in when

the whole world has gone out."

*What seems to*

*grow fairer to me as life goes by*

*is the love and the grace and tenderness of it;*

*not its wit and cleverness and grandeur of knowledge—*

*grand as knowledge is—but just the laughter of*

*children and the friendship of friends, and the*

*cozy talk by the fire, and the sight of flowers,*

*and the sound of music.*

ANONYMOUS

*You can make more
friends in two months by becoming
interested in other people than you can in two
years by trying to get other people interested in you.*

DALE CARNEGIE

*The friendships which last are those wherein each
friend respects the other's dignity to the
point of not really wanting
anything from him.*

CYRIL CONNOLLY

*Never while I keep
my senses shall I compare
anything to the delight of a friend.*

HORACE

*In friendship we find nothing false or insincere;
everything is straightforward, and springs from the heart.*

CICERO

*I can never think of promoting my
convenience at the expense of a friend's
interest and inclination.*

GEORGE WASHINGTON

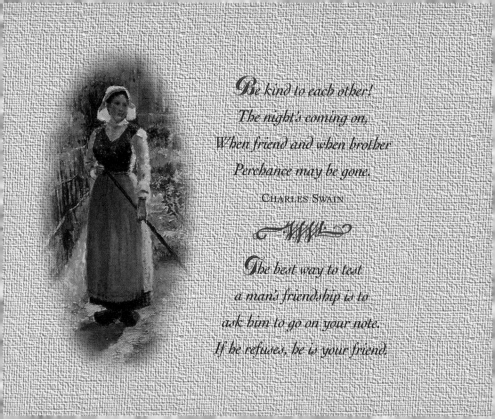

*Be kind to each other!*
*The night's coming on,*
*When friend and when brother*
*Perchance may be gone.*

CHARLES SWAIN

*The best way to test*
*a man's friendship is to*
*ask him to go on your note.*
*If he refuses, he is your friend.*

It is a noble and great thing
to cover the blemishes and
excuse the failings of a friend;
to draw a curtain before his stains,
and to display his perfections;
to bury his weaknesses in silence,
but to proclaim his virtues
upon the housetop.

SOUTH

# No Friend Like an Old Friend

There is no friend like the old friend

who has shared our morning days,

No greeting like his welcome,

no homage like his praise;

Fame is the scentless sunflower,

with gaudy crown of gold;

But friendship is the breathing rose,

with sweets in every fold.

OLIVER WENDELL HOLMES

# The Best Treasure

There are veins in the hills where jewels hide
And gold lies buried deep;
There are harbor-towns where the great ships ride,
And fame and fortune sleep;
But land and sea though we tireless rove,
And follow each trail to the end,
Whatever the wealth of our treasure-trove,
The best we shall find is a friend.

JOHN F. MOMENT

*Little* do men perceive what solitude is, and
how far it extendeth. For a crowd is not company,
and faces are but a gallery of pictures, and talk but
a tinkling cymbal, where there is no love.

FRANCIS BACON

*Three* men are my friends: he that loves me, he that
hates me, and he that is indifferent to me. Who loves me
teaches me tenderness. Who hates me teaches me caution.
Who is indifferent to me teaches me self-reliance.

THESE TIMES

"*Stay*" is a charming word in a friend's vocabulary.

AMOS BRONSON ALCOTT

*A* doubtful friend is worse than a certain enemy.
Let a man be one thing or the other,
and we then know how to meet him.

AESOP

*L*ife is partly what we make it,
and partly what it is made
by the friends whom we choose.

TEHYI HSIEH

*True friends*

*don't spend time*

*gazing into each other's eyes.*

*They may show great tenderness toward*

*each other, but they face in the same direction —*

*toward common projects, interests,*

*goals — above all, toward a*

*common Lord.*

C. S. LEWIS

There are good ships, and there are bad ships,
but the best ships are friendships.

Love demands infinitely less than friendship.

GEORGE JEAN NATHAN

Friend who suffereth alone doth his friend offend.

JEAN DE ROTROU

*Reprove a friend in secret, but praise him before others.*

ANONYMOUS

*The only thing to do is to
hug one's friends tight and do one's job.*

EDITH WHARTON

*One's friends are that part of the human race
with which one can be human.*

GEORGE SANTAYANA

With every friend I love

who has been taken into

the brown bosom of the earth

a part of me has been buried there;

but their contribution to my being of happiness,

strength and understanding remains

to sustain me in an

altered world.

HELEN KELLER

$\mathcal{M}$y coat and I live
comfortably together. It has
assumed all my wrinkles, does not hurt
me anywhere, has moulded itself on my deformities,
and is complacent to all my movements, and I only
feel its presence because it keeps me warm.
Old coats and old friends
are the same thing.

VICTOR HUGO

*Nothing will so much delight the mind*
*as a faithful and pleasing friendship.*
*How great a good is it when the hearts are prepared,*
*wherein a man may safely bury all his secrets,*
*whose conscience thou fearest less than thy own,*
*whose words may terrify thy discontents,*
*whose counsel can resolve thy doubts,*
*whose mirth may dissipate thy sorrow,*
*and whose countenance may comfort thee.*

SENECA

# The Earth Grows Glad

A friend is one in whose presence you may not know how or why, you find comfort and satisfaction. You like to be with him or her. The mere sense of contiguity is a delight. Other people come and other people go, and you do not care; but, when this person comes, sunshine comes, the air is clearer, there is more life in it, the flowers grow more beautifully, the sky is fairer, and the night is deeper. All the earth grows glad; and there is a new note in the song of the birds.

M. J. SAVAGE

The only good teachers
for you are those friends
who love you, who
think you are interesting
or very important,
or wonderfully funny.

BRENDA UELAND

O Friendship! thou fond
soother of the human breast,
to thee we fly in every calamity.

OLIVER GOLDSMITH

He who expects his friend
not to be annoyed at his wens
will excuse the other's warts.
It is only fair that one who
asks indulgence for shortcomings
should give it in return.

HORACE

*Tis something to be willing
to commend; but my best praise
is that I am your friend.

THOMAS SOUTHERNE

*When friends stop being frank*

*and useful to each other,*

*the whole world*

*loses some of its radiance.*

ANATOLE BROYARD

*Do not save your loving speeches*

*For your friends till they are dead;*

*Do not write them on their tombstones,*

*Speak them rather now instead.*

ANNA CUMMINS

*Friendship is
usually treated by the majority
of mankind as a tough and everlasting
thing which will survive all manner of
bad treatment. But this is an exceedingly
great and foolish error; it may die in
an hour of a single unwise word.*

MARIE LOUISE DE LA
RAMÉE (OUIDA)

*It is only the great-hearted who can be true friends.
The mean and cowardly can never know
what true friendship means.*

CHARLES KINGSLEY

*Instead of a gem or a flower, cast the gift
of a lovely thought into the heart of a friend.*

GEORGE MACDONALD

*Friendship is one of the sweetest joys of life.
Many might have failed beneath the bitterness
of their trial had they not found a friend.*

CHARLES HADDON SPURGEON

*However well proven a friendship may appear,*
*there are confidences that it should not hear;*
*and sacrifices which should not be required of it.*

JOSEPH ROUX

*The death of a friend is equivalent to the loss of a limb.*

GERMAN PROVERB

*Be slow in choosing a friend, slower in changing.*

BENJAMIN FRANKLIN

# Tell Him So

If you have a word of cheer

That may light the pathway drear;

Of a brother pilgrim here,

Let him know.

Show him you appreciate

What he does, and do not wait

*Till the heavy hand of fate*

*Lays him low.*

*If your heart contains a thought*

*That will brighter make his lot,*

*Then, in mercy, hide it not;*

*Tell him so.*

J. A. EGERTON

*If a friend is in trouble,*

*don't annoy him by asking*

*if there is anything you can do.*

*Think up something*

*appropriate and do it.*

EDGAR WATSON HOWE

# All the Best

Then speak no ill, but lenient be

To others' failings as your own.

If you're the first a fault to see,

Be not the first to make it known;

For life is but a passing day;

No lips can tell how brief the stay.

Be earnest in the search of good,

And speak of all the best we may.

*After an acquaintance of ten minutes*
*many women will exchange confidences that*
*a man would not reveal to a lifelong friend.*

PAGE SMITH

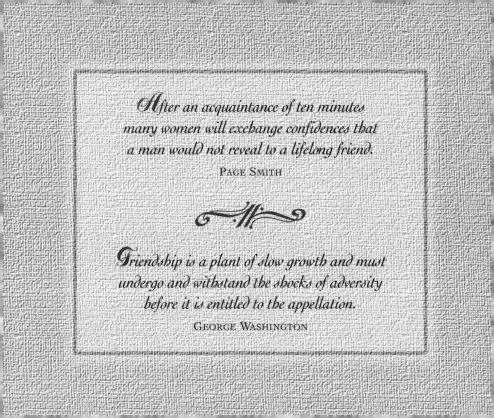

*Friendship is a plant of slow growth and must*
*undergo and withstand the shocks of adversity*
*before it is entitled to the appellation.*

GEORGE WASHINGTON

# Forget Me Not

But oh, if grief thy steps attend,
If want, if sickness be thy lot,
And thou require a soothing friend,
Forget me not! forget me not!

MRS. OPIE